An Apple Is Just a Bird with No Beak

An Apple Is Just a Bird with No Beak

Poetry & Prose by

Bobbie Dumas Panek

© 2025 Bobbie Dumas Panek. All rights reserved.
This material may not be reproduced in any form, published,
reprinted, recorded, performed, broadcast,
rewritten, or redistributed without
the explicit permission of Bobbie Dumas Panek.
All such actions are strictly prohibited by law.

Cover design by John N. Panek
Cover image by Eric Shute

ISBN: 978-1-63980-756-7

Kelsay Books
502 South 1040 East, A-119
American Fork, Utah 84003
Kelsaybooks.com

Acknowledgments

Thank you to the following publication, in which a version of this poem previously appeared:

What We See On Our Journeys: An anthology of poetry by Onondaga County poets and poets that support Onondaga County poetry: "Lovely Locks"

Bobbie would like to thank the writing groups that have helped her hone her skills and strengthen her writing: Finger Lakes Writing Group, Wonderful Women Writers, Palace Poetry, and the Peeps, a small circle of writing friends. Special thanks to Sr. Constance Marie, her eighth-grade teacher, who encouraged her writing. And thanks to the Auburn Citizen where she wrote a column about raising four children on a dairy farm and to Downtown Books and Coffee who helped her to publish these stories as: "Just Another Day." Finally, FootHills Publishing agreed to publish, "Morning Walks: Zen Mediations," and special gratitude to Karen Kelsay at Kelsay Books for publishing this book. Bobbie appreciates all her good friends and fellow wordsmiths.

Contents

Part One

Umbilical Cord	15
Royal Innocence	17
Cigarettes and Lace	18
Laundry Shelf	19
boys with longing lure shy girls	20
Lovely Locks	21

Part Two

on losing my husband of 46 years when he died in his sleep from a heart attack.	25
Remember	26
Voyage	29
Moving from Center	30
Dairy Farmer	31
Mid-June	32
Lunch	33
Lawns	34
Flower Beds	35
Quiet	36
Loneliness	37
No One to Share It With	38
Fear	39
August 19, 2022	40
September 11, 2022—Dim Lot	41
October 4, 2022	42
Beethoven's 9th Symphony	43

Part Three

Screw It—11/27/22	47
Death Happened	48
Survivors' Guilt	49
November 23, 2022	50

Part Four

I Yearn	53
On-line Dating: A Caveat	54
Grief and More Grief: A Difference in Perception	55
this is about the guy who is losing his memory	56
I'm seventy-two years old and my heart is breaking	57
Notes in Hollow Spaces	58
Souls Familiar Seek Each Other	59
September 24, 2024 (To My Boyfriend)	60
October 19, 2024	61
(Boyfriend)	62
Day Is Closing	63

Part One

Umbilical Cord

Assume the position. Babies in utero breathing fluid—
how does that work? Why can't we continue
to breathe in water? Did valves/gills open
and close like heating vents in my cellar?

Memories of family parties: haze
of cigarette smoke, ashtrays, tinkling glasses,
different sizes for whiskey sours, martinis, old fashions,
scotch on the rocks. I was schooled.

Cocktail parties at our house—important
for a politician. Chair burned one time
in our living room. Some big-shot was in town.
My parents had a party for the congressman,
representative, or governor. A cigarette
between the cushion and the chair and the gold
brocade melted. Smoke filled the house.
Someone carried the burning chair outside.
Insurance guy came to get a report. We were told
what to say and what not to say.
What is the truth? Yours or mine?

Our family didn't travel. Too many kids.
Not enough money. Interrupted conversations—
too much talk—rhetoric—same same—we didn't
travel to new places. Needle stayed
stuck like on a 33 rpm.

Breakfast: cream of wheat, oatmeal.
What were those haystacks called?
Those rectangles? Shredded wheat.
Oh my God, needed so much sugar
and milk. Could scratch your throat
to smithereens if they weren't soggy.
Strange, this human form we carry around.
Began breathing in water then forgot how.
We only want to go back to the spirit side.
This human business, bristles like shredded
wheat. I hear a poem and wonder if it's written
by a man or a woman. I'd wager a woman.
The language sounds melodious, thoughtful,
connected—
like the umbilical cord, sound of a heartbeat,
water rushing smooth and soft.

Royal Innocence

1963, Beckie and I made thirty-five cents an hour babysitting. On our way home from 7th grade, we'd stop at J.J. Newberry's, buy a pound of jelly beans in "two separate bags please." With our white, waxed sacks of sweet, colorful jewels, we'd saunter the mile home, getting higher and higher on sugar. Talk about royalty, I now have Nine Crowns.

Cigarettes and Lace

Tall, white, metal cabinet in our kitchen
contained Mom's Old Golds, Dad's white carton
of Kents beside the church envelopes on the top shelf.

Next shelf down, held missals, mostly black with red-edged pages, some falling apart, others—small white 1st Communion missals, those mostly for show. They had pictures of smiling white priests, their brown hair—perfectly parted. Children were dressed to perfection, gleaming smiles, crisp outfits.

Another shelf was for mantillas
black or white lace, large triangles
or small circles.

We'd bobby-pin one to the top of our heads, before entering Church. Before we piled into the car, we each tried to pass Dad's inspection. We rarely passed. *My slip was showing. Why didn't I iron my dress? Didn't I know there was a spot on the front? Why didn't we kids ever polish our shoes?* Each Sunday, we'd parade down the center aisle and kneel near the altar. I always prayed for God to make me acceptable.

Laundry Shelf

Our family of ten lived in a stately brick house
with white, brick arched windows. Pushing open
the heavy front door, visitors met a wide, winding
staircase, lined with gracious, curved wall.
Dining room had corner cabinets. One holding
a heavy, black dial phone with the longest, curled
phone cord, needed for a house with eight girls
from 3 to 18. Busy home. Dad—a politician,
golfer, hunter, bowler, Elks, Kiwanis. Often out
campaigning, or at one of his clubs.

Mom—Busy. Raised us. Fixed meals, helped
with homework. Did the laundry—a mountain—
which sluiced down a chute from the master bathroom.
Clothes flowed to the first floor, tucked underneath
that long staircase. Small chute door was on the right,
dryer straight ahead, washer on the left. Just enough room
for Mom to stand and pivot. Everything handy
including the bottle of vodka well hidden
behind the large cardboard cylinder
of All powdered detergent.

boys with longing lure shy girls

The lake—a shell with tiny pebbles, my toes sink down
into scratchy sand. Churning movement brings me closer
to memories hidden, screeching up from depths of thoughts buried.

Drunken beach parties, murmurs, overheard in the Popcorn Shop
on Saturday nights. Teens pile into cars, convoy to Mountain View.
Circle bonfires blaze. Hold hands, hug, kiss, drink beer, smoke
   cigarettes.

Whispers, strolls, eventual romps in the woods where boys with
   longing
lure shy girls with promises. Babies are made on summer nights in
   the 60s.
As the lake returns flotsam to the shore along with seaweed—legs
   are tangled.

            Water holds the promise of cleansing.
               Teen girls get wet, realize
                  depths are deceptive.

Lovely Locks

On my morning walk, I think about a woman from church. Each Sunday I'd be envious of her coif. When my parents visited my father commented, "Oh Bobbie, isn't that woman striking? Look at her beautiful hair." Even though Mom, Mary Frances McCabe, sat right between us, Dad loved to point out attractive women. Years later, I realize that "that" woman had been wearing a wig. All that envy, feeling less-than, me with less-than vibrant hair, even if I'd stuffed it with jello—it wouldn't be thick, luscious, curly like hers. I took my jealousy, pent-up, inferior emotions, rolled them up into a hairnet, and tossed it all high into a pine tree. Now it sits—soft and thick, a lovely home for baby squirrels.

Part Two

on losing my husband of 46 years when he died in his sleep from a heart attack.

cracked eggs
heart split open
colorful, scattered, shattered, plastic pieces
in the park, on the grass, left over from the hunt
i put shards in my pocket and carry them home
easter birth with new beginnings for him and for me
forty-six years of marriage cremated
spring—new life
just like that
start anew
as if a season creates in me a willingness
without grief, longing, confusion
at the table we are all gathered
well, not all of us
one person significantly not there
he'd been reborn, we'd been robbed.
remember?
grandchildren ask
ooma, what's with the cracked eggs

i'd put them on a glass butter dish in the center of the table

i said
those represent easter eggs

my son-in-law said
oh, I thought it was pieces to a puzzle

Yes

Remember

Thursday May 5th, 2022

Swimming in murky water
What is in my way
Who do I trust
Clumsy on land. I spill water

Friday May 6th, 2022

Dizzy when I wake up. When I bend down to hook up Abby to go out, I nearly keel over. On my way to turn in license plates for Greg's car, I notice flowering trees: pink, raspberry. Greg evaporated. My ten-year-old grandson, Ryan, asked my daughter the night before PaPa's wake, what to expect. She explained the way we'd line up, and said people would come through offering condolences, and that PaPa's ashes would be in a box. Ryan said, "Mom, do we have to watch PaPa burn?"

May 7, 2022

Last night after mowing the lawn I called Penny. I'd been worried that they were away, and it made me sad. And I thought the neighbors beside me (Kate and Ben) were gone, and it made me sad. And I could see that Luanne's car was gone. So everyone around me was gone. I felt so alone. I then watched Penny pull into her garage and I called her. She was friendly but had no idea how sad I was. She talked calmly, and I could barely talk. I knew I'd cry, so I said I had to go. And then I cried. I sat on the couch with

Abby, held her tight and told her my thoughts. Then I talked to Greg. I asked him, did it hurt? Did he feel alone as he traveled away from his bed? Greg didn't like doing things alone. I pictured Greg on his side in bed with his left hand up near the pillow. His eyes closed and his heart stopped. Was he awake when it stopped? Was he high as an eagle when he met God? Did he feel any pain first? Tears slid down my face. Not in torrents. But in slow motion. Each tear from each eye followed the other, knowing the way. I felt loss. I felt confusion and fear. So now I'm alone. Each day I'll make decisions about my life only. What I'll eat when. Where I'll go when. When I wake.

May 13, 2022

I'm sitting at my new accountant's office. He and his right arm gal are going over my paperwork and getting things put into place. 11 a.m. They are poring over financial statements. I feel like crying. It's as if any minute I will fall apart. They are so kind, professional. My life is like a giant jigsaw puzzle. They are finding the corners, and flat edges, to put the borders together. My mind is swirling in muddy water. Their gates are open. Mine are filled with seaweed.

May 19, 2022

I found the Tree of Heaven growing in my garden two months after Greg passed away. Now, this ought to have been a good omen. Right? No, there's a catch. The Tree of Heaven has a common name: Tree of Hell. But wait, how is that possible? The plant is an invasive species also referred to as Chinese Sumac. It invades septic systems, infrastructures, and sidewalks. This first perceived delightful specimen has a dark side. Like Dr. Jekyll and Mr. Hyde, it's oppositional. On the surface a thin, pretty stem. Silently, it travels with deep intent, controlling as much as possible.

Memorial Day 2022

While mowing the grass beneath the apple trees, I notice something sitting on a branch in the tree. I wonder what it is. An apple or a bird? I look closer, all around its shape for a beak. It's an apple. I decide—an apple is a bird without a beak.

June 13, 2022

I don't know when I will die or how I will die. I do know—with conviction—eventually I'll die and re-join the spirit world where I started. It will be familiar. Often, I crave being underwater, surrounded by fluid. I want to feel that soft pressure against my face, my head, my body. All of me remembers being jostled, rocked inside a pressurized closed system of life. I remember and return there when I meditate, tucked safely back in my embryonic state.

Voyage

He was my anchor—rusty, clanky, hard to handle with sharp edges.
He kept our boat stable. Sure, there were big winds, and storms.
We picked up anchor, and moved our boat to a new home behind
the orchard. He watered flowers/vegetables outside. I watered
thirty-something inside plants. He mowed the four acres.
I cleaned the big house. He plowed snow. I got groceries.
We shared our dog. He played tug-of-war with her.
I took her for walks. He pulled weeds around the fruit trees.
I paid the bills, balanced the checkbooks.

He liked to bake. I mailed the birthday cards. Now and then
we played cards or had friends in for apple crunch. I was in groups.
He watched news and sports. We argued a lot. He had a hard time
telling the truth. I wasted money at thrift shops. He didn't trust
doctors. I'd worked in the medical field. I liked to read and write.
He liked to antagonize. I liked quiet. He liked chronic news.
He liked staying home. I liked travel adventures.
He teased children. I took them on nature trails.
His anchor kept us afloat for forty-six years.

Often, I wanted to jump ship. Occasional mutiny on deck.
Our four children, always our lifeboats. Our eight grandchildren,
inflatable rafts. Our dog Abby, our radio. I was seasick
with each pregnancy. His three back surgeries took away
his vigor. We rode rough waters, survived the gales.
On March 15, 2022, asleep in his berth, God whispered,
"C'mon Captain, it's time to go home."
I'm adrift without an anchor.
And it keeps raining.

Moving from Center

What is the date today? What day is it? How long has it been? How long have I been off track, like the big heavy door of the old carriage barn with two doors which run out from center, held on by century-old, rusty tracks. Their wheels stubborn to move, no longer greased. Their passage interrupted by cedar needles, broken pieces of shingles, debris left by squirrels. They would just as soon leave the track as stay on it. I'd be in a fix to try to keep the giant door from completely falling off. At times I'd leave it in a precarious position, run down to the barn, yell to Greg, "Hey, when you get a chance, please fix the carriage house door." I thought we'd left that problem behind when we built the ranch house—near the orchard—after selling the farm. Now Greg is gone. My sense of time keeps falling off the track.

Dairy Farmer

a persona poem

I've a right to be angry, and you would too,
if you were me, and I were you. I worked hard all my life.
My Ma died when I was young, and it sure stung.
Milked cows, cleaned stalls, cleaned out the gutter.
All the while, missing my mother. I prayed for her to live.
Made promises to God. He didn't listen.
We covered her with sod. Now my body's weak,
and my back can't take the strain. How'd you like
to be always in pain? I've a wife and family; they want me
to be kind. I would, if I could, with a different mind.
I'm rough and gruff, and mostly mean. As though I have
a slate to wipe clean. Wish I could start over, begin anew.
This time, I know what I'd do. Drive Ma to Roswell Park
or Cleveland Clinic. Forget about the cows and chicks.
Would have stayed with her through thick and thin.
Made sure she was made whole again.
Things could've been different had I taken a stand.
But it was a different time. I was barely a man. Ya.
I'm set in my ways, a lot like my Pa.
You would be too, if you'd lost your Ma.

Mid-June

My mode of operations was blaming. Blaming Greg because I wasn't happy. Blaming Pop because I wasn't happy. Blaming my friend because I wasn't happy. And now that Pop is gone, Greg is gone, and I'm aware (woke), I can't blame anybody. I have to figure out how—to be happy, when I want to eat, how much I want to sleep? What I want to do, or don't want to do? What do I want to read? Who do I want to hang out with? Do I want to meditate, do Tai Chi, watercolor? I get to choose. I have ultimate freedom. If I want to be happy it's my job. It's on me. Abby and I get along famously. We love each other very much. But we also have to get used to being apart because when I get home after being gone for a few hours she's ballistic happy to see me. Makes me feel good. But it would be nice to get her into a doggy daycare. Someplace where she can go, and get worn out, have fun, and know I'll come and pick her up. It would be good for both of us. Heading out now to mow the back yard. Can't blame anybody.

Lunch

He cooked lunch, our big meal. I was so tired of meat, potatoes, and vegetables. I wanted soup/salad, tuna casserole with chopped celery and onions. Every morning he'd ask what kind of potatoes I wanted: "Mashed, boiled, or fried?" I'd say, "I'm tired of potatoes." He'd say, "So you cook." I'd say, "Mashed. Please." Now I eat salad, almond butter on a banana, cereal, quesadillas, repeat. I miss mashed potatoes.

Lawns

Yes. I can mow the lawns. Yes. I'm capable. Yes, it takes me three hours on the riding mower. Yes, I bought a weed whacker. Yes, that takes me about two hours. Yes, I've hired a snowplow service for the winter. But I'll need to shovel out the front yard for Abby's daily business.

Flower Beds

They are okay but would certainly appreciate watering. I pull weeds, but they return as I walk back to the house.

Quiet

Yes, there's quiet in this house. So much quiet. A voice in my head asks, "So what are you going to do now?" I water the plants and put in a load of laundry. The voice says, "Now, what are you going to do?" I look at Abby and say, "We'll go for a walk after lunch." The voice says, "What are you going to fix for lunch?" I want to yell at the voice and scream, Will you just STOP. Stop watching me! But I turn to Abby and tell her, "I'm going to make tuna fish with chopped celery. How does that sound?"

Loneliness

I tell stories to people who are not listening. Like my chiropractor, when I hurt my shoulder, he truly did not care. He interrupted my tale constantly and told me to try different postures. But I wanted to share how I slept in the gazebo on a thin mattress with my grandsons:10 years old and 6 years old. They are from Southern California and have never slept outdoors. The Doctor asked, "How far up your back can you reach with your left hand?"

No One to Share It With

I saw a fox on the side of the road
on my way to an appointment. A beautiful,
wonderful, wild fox. Grey with tan and blue
streaks. Strolling confidently along the field
unaware of me. His long tail pointed straight
out. A gift. Spiritual. Significant. For me.
A moment. Only mine.

Fear

What to do with all the apples when they begin to fall? I don't want to worry. I'm learning to live one day at a time. But I know how much time my husband spent with Abby picking up those fallen apples. And how much time they spent picking apples from the trees. Bushels upon bushels. The past two years, bumper crops of organic apples. How will I keep up?

August 19, 2022

Looks like I'm going be one of those seventy-year-old women, who sits in a rocker, on her front porch, doing crossword puzzles, while drinking iced, blueberry-creamed coffee. Crickets chirp, a rooster crows, a dog barks, and sheriffs' cars whine with sirens screaming, Get Out Of My Way. Since Greg died, I'm learning my way, alone, as a widow, no longer a couple. I no longer have someone here to notice if I'm dead or alive. Meals are catch-can; pizza from Byrne's dairy, salad with a can of tuna dumped on top, carrots and hummus, banana with almond butter. It's okay. I eat okay. It's summertime. Who wants a hot meal when it's above 90°? Slowly, I'm getting used to my new life, living alone. My thinking is still loud. Abby enjoys Hoopes Park more than I do. She's sociable and loves to smell everything. She gets frequent pats on the head while people chant, "Oh, what a sweet dog. She's so soft. She's so friendly." Abby thinks she's the prettiest dog in town. I want exercise. I don't want to stop every few minutes to smell the area. I want to pray the rosary, and walk in earnest. Abby makes frequent stops to roll on the grass, to plop down under a shade tree to just enjoy the coolness. I stand in the sun, waiting for her to release me from her leash. As I sit in this rocker, I again hear the neighbor's rooster crow. It baffles me. Why is it crowing now? It isn't dusk yet. Or maybe for him, low to the ground, behind a hedge, it is. Earlier five sheriffs' cars went wailing up our road, then within an hour a S.A.V.E.S. ambulance came wailing back down. Something awful occurred up the road on this benign, August, late afternoon, with people expecting the same old— same old. That's the way life unfolds. We don't know what's coming around the curve. Greg left oh so suddenly. Without a word, or a moan, or a glance. He just slipped away in the night like a ship, quiet and elusive.

September 11, 2022—Dim Lot

I left my car in the small, dimly lit parking lot. Surrounded by bushes, close to downtown, close to the railroad tracks. I'm nervous. Two men stand behind the senior center smoking cigarettes. Grey cloudy wisps curled over their heads in the evening air. Their voices lower as I walk back to my car with Abby, my sweet dog, on her leash. All ten pounds of her, alert. She hesitates when we get to my Ford Escape. Usually, she goes to the back door, waits for me to lift her up. But she stays back. I say, "C'mon Abby, let's go." Reluctantly, she slowly sniffs the ground. Then, I pick her up, put her in the back seat, and notice how sticky my door handle is. I get in the car and quickly lock the doors. I want to leave the dim parking lot as soon as possible. I breathe easier when I get to the Arterial, with streetlights, and cars moving beside me. In the morning, I go to the car to get something from the front passenger seat. That door handle is also ridiculously sticky.

October 4, 2022

But silence is certain. That's why I write. I'm alone and I write. No, I'm not alone. There's someone here who trembles.
　　　　　—Alejandra Pizarnik, "Paths of the Mirror"

Why do some of us have this burning in our minds, hearts, and fingers, to find paper, pens, typewriter, a tablet? Why do we love shopping where writing supplies fill the aisles? Because we tremble. And we will tremble until we get our stories down. We will feel the wrenching in our insides, our scratchy inside walls, until we soothe the rash. Words are balm. Poems and stories are the remedy. Not for everyone. No. Others are soothed with television. My husband needed news all day long, only interrupted for sports. Those were the whispers calling to him. Give him a sensational tragedy: a school shooting, a hurricane, and he was attached—moment by moment. Other people need gambling, sex, alcohol, drugs. They have a hunger inside which requires quieting, numbing, with neon flashing lights and beeps, musical scales to tighten the drive, orgasms to remove them from the planet for moments at a time, altering chemicals and products to silence their minds. We all tremble for something. Buddhists teach themselves to find their tremble, their trouble, to root it out, open it, see it, observe it, let it pass. They've learned to say, *There now. I see what you want. I understand why you're thinking. It's okay. Thinking is okay. But move along now. Get back to that other place where you don't need a thing.*

Beethoven's 9th Symphony

Today, I saw the flash of a grey squirrel—followed by the quickening of a small red squirrel. Then, as we rounded the curve, a red cardinal flew into the woods. A big deer with wide antlers strutted off and another deer flew by, its white tail high. I smelled the acrid aroma of a skunk, then watched another deer fly through the woods, oblivious to branches.

I heard in Beethoven's 9th Symphony—that lapse where the thread is nearly out—about to drop, and miraculously re-knits more music, from the needles of Beethoven's mind. It stopped again for a split infinity, then resumed as if saying, What? I was only catching my breath.

Her husband died silently, and she stayed stalled in the house and in her heart. Sisters died tragically. One person sat stoned on their front porch—out of it—unable to speak. He died in the factory—all lines stopped. She went out dancing. A child died from SIDS, and the babysitter became an addict. He died young of a rare syndrome. His mother wrote books. Another mother moved to Iceland.

My blister shed its skin three times. That's how pronounced it was. Pure stress. A good friend visited me. We tried to right some wrongs while walking on the railroad bed. My dog, Abby, stopped us often with her instinctive sniffing. We found a mangled dog beside a make-shift grave. Garish. Gory. An empty Pampers box, a bouquet of ugly plastic flowers jammed into the ground, beside a giant red Christmas tree bulb. To signify what? What had happened to that poor animal? What other animal attacked it so fiercely? And where were the people who were mid-burial when we appeared? This scene added to the already escalating—heated discussion. My lips begging for water. For peace.

When we arrived home, I immediately drank a large, cold glass of tap water. But the stress had already taken hold. The blister had seeded and settled. Our attempt at civility, and understanding, was hard to come by. My husband had died. She wanted to support me. But instead gave me strict orders, "Do not use my husband for advice on things."

"Okay. Got it." The man I'd known for fifty years and enjoyed hanging out with was now relegated to the married side of the tracks. I'd been kicked to the curb. Now a widow, also known as threat. Okay. Got it. Hey, thanks for your support.

She went home. I applied lip cream for seventeen days. Lost three layers of lip. Finally near normal. I don't know what happened to the half-eaten dog. I don't know why becoming a widow pushes me off the train.

Watch me spread my wings. The things I can do without a straitjacket. The things I can say with a microphone. The tighter you pull my boundaries, the more urgent my need to fly. Watch me. Tape my mouth shut. I will learn sign language. Don't restrain me.

Part Three

Screw It—11/27/22

My hair is falling out. Stress. Lip blister won't heal. Stress. Buy food for one. Stress. Troubleshoot when furnace quit on 11/15. Put new batteries in thermostat, changed filter, turned furnace on/off, called service. Guy comes on 17th. Yesterday 26th it stopped. Today, it's 60 degrees in the house. Stress. Recently removed outside hoses. Turned off water valves in basement. Found PVC pipe to make sewer vent taller for winter. I'm weary. Cold. Pissed off. So tired of this. My husband died eight months ago. Regardless of what you think I feel, I know what I feel. I don't feel like explaining anything to you about anything. I've managed Abby, and the yard, the orchard, my loneliness, the holidays, with no one to ask how I slept, no one to fix me a hot meal, no one to watch Abby so I can hike, or bike, or visit others for any length of time. It's all on me now. Well guess what? I'm done playing games. Mark will troubleshoot the furnace. The Cider guy will come tomorrow to put up motion detector lights. The furnace guy will come back. I will continue anti-anxiety and anti-depression medicine. I will continue with my counselor. Please just leave me alone stress. I'm done. This business is over. This stress. I'll figure out how to stay mindful, creative, at peace.

Death Happened

Death happened. Snuck into this house on the Ides of March and scooped him up. He floated up, and out, and I haven't seen him since. How odd, understanding death. What do we compare it to? We haven't experienced death. How are we to describe it? We only feel the void, absence. The rest is built on faith, what we've read, heard, believe. But we cannot know. Not with absolute knowledge. Yet, after he died, he did talk to me through a psychic. He sounded like Greg. He talked like Greg. He told me things the psychic would not have known him to say. So I believe his soul has left his body. And his soul can communicate with me. My father also talked to me through the psychic. He'd struggled with death. He was so afraid. He clutched at each rasp of breath. We encouraged him, "Dad, it's okay. You can go. You'll be fine."

Dad later told me, "Dying wasn't that hard." He said, "It was just like going into another room." So that kind of dying—in a bed, in a rehab, at the age of ninety-five, makes perfect sense to me. But it was the other—the theft at night, in the dark, while we were sleeping. And then I was okay with it. Seeing Greg in his bed—I knew he was happy by his peaceful face. He was fortunate that God took him in his bed, in his home, while he was sleeping.

I wonder
was he awake at all
was it dream-like or a cogent reality
was there a question and did he answer
did he hear Spoken words,
see a light to follow
a path
a flight?

His body cold, I knew he was gone—taken.

Survivors' Guilt

Maybe I have survivor's guilt. I don't really know what it means. All I know is, I'm still here. And he isn't. I'm alive, but he died. So I get to tell the story. I get to frame it. I'm not sure that's fair. But that's the way it works. We met on a blind date. We had a quick relationship. I was heading out of town. He convinced me to stay. I needed another place to live. We got engaged. I moved in with him and his father. We got married. All of that took place within six months. We started a family and were blessed with four amazing children. I found it difficult to live with his father. He was a tough man.

We had fun on the farm. Greg worked very hard. Pop worked hard. After 10 years staying home, I went back to work, and Greg and Pop sold the cows. Now Greg was the stay-at-home dad. He cash-cropped and watched the kids. Sometimes the kids were stuck in the house with Pop. He was grouchy. After Pop died, the kids started college in a long line: Sarah at Union and UB, Laura at Geneseo, Scott at CCC and Brockport, John at OCC and Syracuse University. Our lives—a series of spirals. Greg with major back problems. Surgeries. Infections. Pain pills. Pain pills. Gabapentin. More Gabapentin. His personality changed. He was angry. Discouraged. Frustrated. Miserable. Our children got married. We were not able to travel. I could, but he couldn't. Things devolved, caved-in, fell apart, threadbare. We sold the farm. We built a ranch house, handicap accessible. It was easier for Greg to get around inside the house, until the neuropathy that had started in his feet—traveled up to his torso, and he began to fall constantly. It was sad to watch him decline. It was hard for me to fully understand him. And hard for him to fully understand me. And who knew? You don't know what to expect. How can you? You just move along, hope things go well. Deal with what is. What is survivors' guilt? It's what I'm feeling.

November 23, 2022

Life is raspy when you are grieving, and you live alone, and it's a holiday. Nerves crackle at checkouts when others have no idea, and they make snarky comments. They don't know how their words land in your empty heart. It's not as if you'll return to a home which welcomes and comforts. Perhaps you hear so few words directed at you, each syllable holds possibility, each tone reverberates. But how are they to know?

Grief
A hollow
A hole
A room for regrets
Longing to understand
Questions without answers

Part Four

I Yearn

I want to move through water, open my mouth, taste krill, jump from an airplane, have the parachute jolt me up, then float down through clouds, deposited upon a field of green. I want to feel the rush of waterfalls, see the shape of the earth from a hot air balloon, to paddle my feet behind me into mud—with only my eyes peering out, to feel all of the pleasurable feelings but none of the painful ones, to sing and harmonize, meditate, connect to the universe, indulge in pleasure without guilt. I want to enjoy riveting, pivotal, fantastical, enduring passion without pain, love without ache, laughter without expense, joy without regret. But it's not possible to live in one continuous orgasmic experience. And so I yearn.

On-line Dating: A Caveat

We met over a year ago online. We fell in love. Took trips to Florida, California, Lake George. We talked, walked, made love, enjoyed movies, theater, farmers markets, biking, hiking, and motorcycling. His short-term memory loss was noticeable. Eventually, tests, scans, labs—prove Alzheimer's. He forgets what we've done, what we've said, and what we've planned. Unfortunately there is no e-harmony return counter. I can't complain to anyone. There was no warranty. There was no "POSSIBLE SIDE EFFECTS" label. There was attraction, laughter, joy, hope for a future. As he moves further away, I fall deeper into despair.

Grief and More Grief: A Difference in Perception

After my husband dies I find a friend online. I feel elation. My son feels betrayal. I feel frustrated. He feels desolation. I see positive change. He says change is difficult. I feel acceptance. He feels enraged. I'm ready to move on. He needs more time. I want to enjoy life. He wants to blame somebody. I want to be happy. He chooses to be miserable. I want him to understand me. He wants me to understand him. I want him to know those forty-six years were hard on me. He was relieved when he and his father finally began a deep relationship. I was weary of verbal abuse and antagonism. He was enjoying their phone conversations. I lived with him for many years while our son had moved across the country. I know my husband was tired of living in his broken body. My son thought we should have found a miracle.

this is about the guy who is losing his memory

He has money, motorcycles, a great sense of humor, a beautiful penis, but he doesn't remember moments we share. I couldn't overlook it. How soon will he forget my name? I had to call it off. Will there be any lingering feeling for me, in his cells? I want happiness. Now. Please. Impossible, I know. Why is life so fucking hard? I'll be okay. He'll be okay. Feeling empty. I'm glad the texts and calls have stopped. I hope he can move on. I hope I can move on. Once he came into my life, he filled it. He filled me. Literally. We became one. We planned all our time together. I began to leave groups . . . slowly. Some were not satisfying. My life is hitting me—in the face—like a hollow whiffle ball, with an annoying whack. My thoughts are loud. My days are long. My life stretches like a barren road. My heart hurts. I didn't seek a man with dementia. A voice inside me questions, could I have waited longer? It felt so dramatic. How much of us was I willing to watch him forget. Too painful. Too scary. Ultimately, I was going to be alone. And now, I am.

I'm seventy-two years old and my heart is breaking

I broke up with a man I love. We've been dating for one year. He's
 sick.
He forgets things. I watch the progression. I worry
about his safety, his choices, wonder
if he should be driving. We live an hour apart.
I am incredibly sad today. I've never self-mutilated
but I think I know what it feels like. I know I need
this break-up. Sweet Jesus, I already miss him.
I'm so sad that he is hurting. Hold him close,
Jesus. Such a long day. It feels like contractions.
Waves keep hitting me, painful waves.

Notes in Hollow Spaces

All seems to be what it's supposed to be. Nature trails lead to lungs, to hearts, to my muse, on my tongue, from the tips of my fingers. Paths in woods near broken stone walls, beside railroad bed, lead to music rushing, under bridges. Notes in hollow spaces, crumbling foundations where industries used the hands of men and women to sort, assemble, box, design. Now moss, roots, abound on logs, side hills, around trees. Ash Borer Beetles decided which trees should be felled. These small insects took down mighty trees—with their tiny teeth and weird bodies. Nothing is ever the same moment to moment. Wind stirs. Waters fall. Shadows dance. Birds chirp. Ants carry heavy loads. Mosquitoes buzz. Dogs pull on leashes. Ivy winds itself up, around, whatever it can. Grows far and wide, even strangles. It's what vines do.

Souls Familiar Seek Each Other

I'm sad. It's so quiet.
The end of a love story.
Her body craves his
misses the oxytocin drip.
Her heart needs a clean cut,
an ablation from the pain.
Knowing his memory lapses
occur more frequently
she's weaning herself
from love's flow
like a baby from mother's milk.
Start with small bites.
Lunch with another widower.
Her therapist says souls
familiar seek each other.
When to cut ties completely
like fallopian tubes, so
nothing can grow?

September 24, 2024 (To My Boyfriend)

Thank you for helping me to find my sensual self, for teaching me to value lovemaking in its purest form. Thank you for wanting me, teaching me to want you, for showing me the art of love I never truly knew. Thank you for teaching me to be vulnerable, feminine, natural, to feel safe, loved, recognized. We enjoyed our wonderful love for over a year. We enjoyed each other: adventures, trains, planes, motorcycles, automobiles. We were booked for a cruise, but we didn't get there. Thank you for your abilities. You helped me so much. So many jobs in my honey-do jar. You enjoyed helping me. Sometimes, we worked together, and we made it fun. I wish you all the best. I wish we could have continued our relationship, but with your Alzheimer's, I knew I was fading from your mind. I wasn't imprinting in your memory. I couldn't do it anymore. It was as if what we did each day, was written on a dry-erase board. Each morning, the board was wiped clean. Perhaps, it makes for a good movie plot, but in real life, it's so darn painful. My love forever, Bobbie.

October 19, 2024

I went to the thrift store to drop off a leather dress, and leather pants I'd bought specifically to surprise him. He owned two Harley-Davidsons. I rode on the back of the trike with him, to a bike rally in Lake George. I also dropped off the sweater jacket he'd bought for me for my birthday. Soon after he bought it for me, he didn't remember buying it. I don't want to see those clothes in my closet. I have no use for them now.

(Boyfriend)

a persona poem

I was told I have Alzheimer's. But I feel
fine. I forget details. Everyone I know over seventy
forgets names, places. What's the big deal? I remember
the important things like who I love. But she doesn't
understand. I've decided to sell my house, one Harley,
most of my belongings, to move into a gradual senior
housing campus. This place is gorgeous. I'll be in a villa
with a garage, patio looking over the school's athletic fields.

I'll get breakfast each morning. Someone to clean
my place twice a month. There are many activities in the main
building: travel opportunities, bus trips, overnight trips, bingo,
fitness groups. I asked my sweetheart to sell her house
and to move in with me. Two of her children live nearby.
We could start fresh. New digs. All new for both of us. I tell her
she won't have to take care of me. I'll already be at a place
where I can get more care. But she's not optimistic like me.
I tried to convince her, but all she does is cry. I'm not eating
much, and I'm losing weight. I haven't been able to sleep
since she ended things. She says I'll forget her. I'll never
forget how she makes me feel. We had over a year
of adventures. So what if I can't keep everything straight
in my head? Big deal if I forget conversations, details
of times together. Why can't she just be happy
that we can be someplace together, safe, no
maintenance, no worries . . . eventually, no memory
of the move, the day, the year, the staff, or even her—
but is that such a big deal? I just want to be happy now.
I want her here with me now. Will that be good enough? Don't
worry about tomorrow. Today is good
enough. I am good enough. Aren't I?
It's crazy. I'm sorry.

Day Is Closing

Light in Western sky descends slow, consistent, persistent. What's between the light and the earth's curve? Words, thoughts, plans, desires live there. Pushed down for another day. Some resurrect in the east. Watch them lift up like daisies or corn. More so when it rains. Puffs of seeds travel on shoes, dogs, wind. Energy moves it all up, or down, across or through. Evening rests each day. Gravity continues in the dark. Water still flows for the blind. Music fades or remains. Sorrows seep deep.

About the Author

Bobbie Dumas Panek is a writer of both poetry and prose and is published in many publications and anthologies. She lives in the Finger Lakes region of New York State and shares her life with four children, their mates, and eight grandchildren. Her dog, Abby, a jumble of white curls, weighs only twelve pounds, but makes all the decisions when they walk in the woods.

Her book, *Morning Walks: Zen Meditations,* can be found at FootHills Publishing. Her second book, *Just Another Day,* can be found on Amazon.

www.ingramcontent.com/pod-product-compliance
Lightning Source LLC
Chambersburg PA
CBHW030914170426

43193CB00009BA/848